GW01246669

Original title:
Arctic Reflections

Author: Swan Charm
ISBN HARDBACK: 978-9916-79-390-9
ISBN PAPERBACK: 978-9916-79-391-6
ISBN EBOOK: 978-9916-79-392-3

Tales of the Frosted Glade

In the whispering woods so serene,
Where shadows dance and glisten bright,
The frost paints silver on the green,
Under the gentle touch of light.

Branches bare with icy lace,
Sparkling gems in morning's breath,
Nature's beauty in still embrace,
A silent dance that conquers death.

Footsteps soft on the frozen ground,
Echoes of stories lost in time,
Every flake a tale unbound,
A symphony in frost and rhyme.

The brook flows gently, crystal clear,
Beneath the veil of winter's guise,
A melody for hearts to hear,
As it reflects the azure skies.

In twilight's glow, the world transforms,
A canvas brushed with quiet grace,
Within the frost, a warmth that warms,
In the glade's heart, a sacred place.

Fractals in the Ice

Patterns bloom like flowers,
In the chill of winter's breath.
Delicate and fleeting,
They dance with subtle grace.

Nature's art emerges,
In the shimmer of the night.
Each crystal tells a story,
Of time caught in stillness.

Reflections weave a tale,
Of beauty stark and bright.
A tapestry of whispers,
Carved within the frost.

Cold fingers reach to trace,
The wonders of the cold.
Infinite repeating shapes,
Unfold in crystal dreams.

Gaze into the silence,
Where magic sparks and sings.
In the fractals found in ice,
Awakens winter's heart.

Mystic Winter's Gaze

In the hush of falling snow,
The world holds its breath so tight.
Moonlight paints the shadows,
On the canvas of the night.

Whispers of the frozen trees,
Echo through the stillness deep.
Mysteries wrapped in silence,
Where ancient secrets sleep.

Stars twinkle like diamonds,
In the velvet sky above.
Each glimmer a reminder,
Of the warmth we dream of.

The air is crisp and biting,
Yet beauty lingers near.
In the grip of winter's chill,
A magic we hold dear.

So let your spirit wander,
In this winter's soft embrace.
For in the mystic stillness,
Lies a timeless, tranquil space.

Frozen Fables

Once upon a winter night,
Stories woven in the frost.
Tales of love and loss and light,
In the chill where time is lost.

Each flake a word of magic,
Drifting down from skies of gray.
Frozen fables gently fall,
Whispered through the snowy play.

The trees stand as guardians,
Their branches draped in white lace.
Holding secrets of the past,
In the quiet, frosty space.

Underneath the icy glaze,
Lie the dreams that once were bold.
Their echoes softly linger,
In the silent, bitter cold.

So listen to the stories,
That the winter winds embrace.
In the frozen fables told,
Find the warmth of winter's grace.

The Stillness of Icebound Dreams

In the cradle of the night,
Where icebound dreams take flight.
The world slows, holds its breath,
In the silence, whispers death.

Moonlight kisses frozen lakes,
Casting shadows long and deep.
Where the stillness gently shakes,
And the heart dares not to weep.

Frost enfolds the sleeping earth,
Like a quilt of silver threads.
In this chill, a quiet birth,
Of dreams woven in soft beds.

Each moment stretched and fragile,
Silhouettes of pale delight.
Time stands still, if only brief,
In the shimmers of the night.

So let the cold caress you,
As you wander through the gleam.
For within the icy stillness,
Lie the pathways of your dream.

Crystalized Silence

In the still of night, whispers freeze,
Stars above like scattered keys.
Quiet moments, time does cease,
In this crystal world, I find my peace.

Snowflakes dance on frosty air,
Each one unique, a whispered prayer.
Echoes softly fade away,
In this silence, I wish to stay.

Moonlight paints the landscape white,
Shadows shifting, pure delight.
Crystal forms in glistening sight,
Wrapped in calm, the world feels right.

Nature's breath, a gentle sigh,
Underneath the slate-gray sky.
Listen close as feelings swell,
In the silence, all is well.

Beneath the Icebound Sky

Beneath the icebound sky I gaze,
Frozen landscapes, a spellbound maze.
Whispers of winter fill the air,
With each flake, a gentle flare.

Silent trees wear coats of white,
Branches stretched, a chilling sight.
Footsteps crunch on crystal ground,
In this frosty silence, peace is found.

Auroras paint the heavens wide,
Colors shifting, colors glide.
Beneath the ice, secrets lie,
In the stillness, dreams can fly.

Each breath a cloud, soft and light,
Embraced by winter's soft invite.
Nature's lullaby, pure and clear,
In this frozen realm, all is near.

The Eternal Chill

The eternal chill wraps all around,
A frosty whisper, a haunting sound.
Winter's breath, crisp and bright,
In this realm, shadows take flight.

Gentle flakes like stars descend,
Covering earth, a white amends.
Timeless beauty, nature's grace,
In this stillness, I find my place.

Frozen lakes of deep blue hue,
Mirror skies, reflecting true.
Each ripple holds a story old,
In the chill, warm tales unfold.

Silver light through branches weaves,
Cradling nights as daylight leaves.
In the heart of winter's glow,
A promise whispered, life will grow.

Northbound Reverie

In a northbound reverie I drift,
Where time is slow, and hearts uplift.
Snowy trails guide the way,
With whispered dreams that sway.

Frosted pines stand tall and proud,
Veiled in mist, a ghostly shroud.
Chasing echoes of the past,
In the silence, spells are cast.

Gentle winds call out my name,
In this wanderlust, I feel no shame.
Beneath the boughs, I find my soul,
In nature's arms, I am made whole.

Stars ignite the velvet night,
Guiding my thoughts, a gentle light.
In this realm where dreams take flight,
Northbound reverie, pure delight.

Celestial Glows

Stars twinkle in the night,
Whispers of ancient light.
Moonbeams dance on silver seas,
Carried softly by the breeze.

Galaxies spin in vast delight,
Painting dark with colors bright.
Nebulas weave their mystic lace,
In the cosmos, a sacred space.

Shooting stars, a fleeting wish,
In the silence, we find bliss.
Constellations guide the way,
Through the night until the day.

Planets roam with silent grace,
In the dark, they find their place.
Celestial wonders, endless skies,
In their glow, our spirits rise.

Infinite dreams, we seek to find,
In the heavens, our hearts unwind.
Boundless beauty, a cosmic song,
In the universe, we all belong.

Windswept Wishes

On the hill, the tall grass sways,
Whispers carried through long days.
Gentle gusts, like lovers' sighs,
Breathe the dreams where freedom lies.

Clouds drift by in endless jade,
Shadows dance in sunlit glade.
Nature's breath, a tender tune,
As the leaves begin to croon.

High above, the kites take flight,
Painting colors in the light.
Every wish that rides the breeze,
Finds a way to soar with ease.

Windswept thoughts take shape and form,
In the storm, we find the calm.
Heartfelt prayers upon the air,
Lifted high without a care.

As the sun sinks low and deep,
In the twilight, secrets keep.
Now the stars lend ear to hear,
Windswept wishes, free from fear.

Frost-gray Canvases

Morning frost on every blade,
Nature's art, a cool cascade.
Silent beauty coats the earth,
In this stillness, we find worth.

Trees adorned with icy lace,
Time stands still in this cold space.
Each twig glistens, a crystal spell,
Whispers of winter, soft farewell.

Pale sunlight breaks the frozen night,
Chasing shadows, welcoming light.
Frost-gray canvases unfold,
Tales of winter softly told.

Footsteps crunch on frozen ground,
Echoes of peace in every sound.
Every breath a puff of mist,
In this beauty, we exist.

With the dusk, a tranquil hue,
Stars awaken, rolling through.
Frost-gray canvases will gleam,
In the stillness, we may dream.

The Edge of Ice

At the brink, where waters freeze,
Silent whispers ride the breeze.
Crystals forming, nature's art,
Chilling beauty, tugging heart.

Waves now still, in quiet breath,
Feeling whispers of the death.
An edge defined by frost and foam,
Leaving warmth far from its home.

Sunset glows in pastel shades,
Merging colors as light fades.
On the edge, the world we see,
A fleeting glimpse of eternity.

Footprints mark the frozen shore,
Stories sung, forevermore.
In this dance of cold and fire,
We find hope, we find desire.

As the night unfurls its cloak,
Crackling ice, the silence broke.
The edge of ice, where dreams arise,
In the dark, we find the skies.

Beneath the Surface

In waters deep where shadows play,
A world unfolds, a hidden sway.
Fish darting swift, secrets to keep,
A gentle lull, the ocean's sweep.

Coral gardens, colors bright,
Life in motion, pure delight.
Echoes dance in liquid dreams,
Nature's pulse in vibrant streams.

Bubbles rise, a whispered song,
In harmony, we all belong.
A fleeting touch, the tide's embrace,
In silence found, a sacred space.

With every wave, a story told,
Of ancient tales and waters cold.
The surface calm, a mirror's face,
Beneath the depths, we find our place.

Blue Hues of Solitude

In shades of blue, the heart reveals,
A canvas soft, where silence feels.
Whispers linger, echoes fade,
The depth of calm, the stillness made.

Oceans vast, horizons wide,
In solitude, I often hide.
Sky and sea, a bond so true,
Reflecting dreams in azure hue.

Waves crash softly on the shore,
Each tide speaks of yearning more.
The vast expanse, a soulful sigh,
Beneath this blue, I learn to fly.

Stars above in velvet night,
Guide my thoughts with distant light.
In solitude, I find my breath,
Among the hues that conquer death.

Chilled Whispers

In winter's breath, the world is still,
Chilled whispers trace the night's cold thrill.
Frosted trees, a crystal gown,
Nature's hush in frosty crown.

In silence deep, the moonlight gleams,
Casting shadows, weaving dreams.
The air is sharp, a biting touch,
Yet in this quiet, I feel so much.

A gentle freeze, a tranquil charm,
Embracing chill, a loving arm.
Each breath a cloud that fades to air,
In frozen stillness, I'm laid bare.

These chilly whispers wrap me tight,
In solitude I find my light.
The world outside, a frosted view,
In winter's grasp, my soul feels new.

Glacial Metaphors

Upon the ice, reflections gleam,
Nature's canvas, cold and cream.
Glaciers move with ancient grace,
Time etched deep in every trace.

In frozen form, a story flows,
Layers speak of time that grows.
Unyielding strength, a silent fight,
In every crevice, caught in light.

Melting slow, a whispered plea,
The change of time, the dance of sea.
Each drip a tale, a fleeting thought,
In glacial forms, wisdom is sought.

Cold beauty cloaked in crystal bright,
Holds the warmth just out of sight.
In metaphors of ice and snow,
Lies the truth of what we know.

Twilight in the Tundra

The sun dips low, a golden hue,
Whispers of night in shades of blue.
Silent echoes through frozen grass,
As shadows lengthen, moments pass.

Stars awaken with twinkling eyes,
Painting dreams across the skies.
The air is crisp, the world asleep,
In twilight's grasp, the secrets keep.

Footprints vanish beneath the snow,
Where the quiet winds gently blow.
Nature's breath, a whispered song,
In this stillness, we all belong.

The horizon glows, a delicate line,
As night embraces the world divine.
In this tranquil, vast expanse,
Life's enigmas hold a chance.

Frozen beauty, a timeless phrase,
In twilight's light, we find our gaze.
Nature's canvas, vast and grand,
Awakens wonders across the land.

Frosty Reveries

In dreams of frost, the world unfolds,
A tapestry of white and gold.
Each flake a whisper, pure and bright,
A dance of crystals in the night.

Frozen whispers adorn the trees,
A symphony carried by the breeze.
The moonlight casts a silver glow,
On frosty fields where shadows flow.

Echoes linger in the chill,
As time slows down, a moment still.
Glittering wonders all around,
In frosty reveries, peace is found.

Joy in silence, soft and deep,
In this realm, our dreams we keep.
Heartbeats echo through the land,
Where every thought is gently planned.

Illusions dance on icy streams,
Weaving through our winter dreams.
In frosty breath, a world anew,
Awaits the heart's unyielding view.

Silence of the Glaciers

In ancient hush, the glaciers lie,
Silent giants 'neath the sky.
Frozen tales of ages past,
In their embrace, time holds fast.

Cracks and crevices softly sigh,
Guarding secrets, whispering why.
The world above, a distant hum,
As icy whispers softly come.

Reflecting light in shades of blue,
A vast expanse of life anew.
Calm serenity, a solemn grace,
In the stillness, we find our place.

The beauty slow, yet fierce and grand,
Shapes of ice shaped by nature's hand.
Let the silence draw you near,
To frozen realms, both bold and clear.

In these depths, the heart can feel,
The pulse of earth, a raw appeal.
The whispers guide through winter's song,
In the glaciers' quiet, we belong.

Dancing with the Northern Wind

A gentle breeze begins to play,
Through the trees in soft ballet.
The northern wind, a wild refrain,
Calls us forth to dance again.

Swirls of snow like feathers fly,
As we move beneath the sky.
In harmony with nature's sound,
Our spirits lifted from the ground.

The rhythms change, both fast and slow,
As icy whispers begin to flow.
With every gust, we twirl and spin,
Embracing all that lies within.

In every chill, a warm embrace,
The northern wind, our timeless grace.
Through frosty laughter, soft and bright,
We find our joy in winter's night.

As dusk descends, the stars ignite,
We dance together, hearts alight.
The northern wind, a fleeting friend,
Whispers secrets that will not end.

Embracing the Chill

Winter's breath upon my face,
Frosted air, a soft embrace.
Tree branches bowed, white with snow,
A world transformed, a quiet glow.

Footsteps crunch on crystal ground,
In this silence, peace is found.
Blankets warm, fire's gentle light,
Embracing the chill, hearts feel right.

The stars above, twinkling bright,
Cold winds sing of winter's night.
A chill that bites, yet brings us close,
In this cold, we find the most.

Hot cocoa steams, laughter shared,
Amongst the frost, love is declared.
Winter's chill wraps us tight,
In its magic, we find delight.

As time whispers, seasons turn,
From the chill, we all will learn.
Embrace the frost, let it in,
A dance of life, where we begin.

Glacial Whispers

Mountains stand with caps of white,
In the dawn, a soft twilight.
Whispers drift through icy air,
Nature's secrets, pure and rare.

Rivers still beneath the freeze,
Echoes rise with gentle ease.
In the silence, shadows play,
Glacial whispers guide the way.

Frozen lakes, a mirror's art,
Reflecting dreams that fill the heart.
Footsteps trace a winding path,
Through the calm and winter's bath.

The quiet hum of nature's song,
In frozen realms, we all belong.
All around, a world so wide,
In glacial whispers, we confide.

As daylight fades, the stars ignite,
With glimmers soft in the night.
Here nature's beauty feels so near,
In glacial whispers, life is clear.

The Dance of Shimmering Lights

Underneath the midnight sky,
Stars above begin to sigh.
Colors burst and softly blend,
In this dance, the night transcends.

Auroras swirl, a magic flight,
Dancing shadows, pure delight.
Whispers of the northern breeze,
Swaying gently through the trees.

Every flicker, every glow,
Nature's art in graceful flow.
Light and dark in sweet embrace,
In this dance, we find our space.

A tapestry of cosmic hue,
Painting dreams in shades so true.
Guided by the moon's soft call,
In shimmering lights, we find it all.

As the night begins to fade,
Memories of magic made.
Hold this moment, let it ignite,
The dance of shimmering lights tonight.

Colors of the Cold

The world adorned in icy lace,
Every flake a unique face.
Winter's palette, cool and bright,
Colors of the cold ignite.

Blues and whites in frosty waves,
Nature's beauty, how it saves.
Ravines deep with soft snow tread,
Painted landscapes, softly spread.

Sunlight kisses the snowy seas,
Glittering crystals in the breeze.
Vibrant hues on every tree,
In cold colors, wild and free.

Glistening paths where shadows lie,
Wrapped in blankets, warm and shy.
Colors dance in the frosty air,
A winter's tale beyond compare.

As seasons change, the warmth will come,
But in this cold, our hearts beat strong.
Embrace the chill in every fold,
Discover joy in colors bold.

Memory of the Icebound Edge

Frozen whispers in the night,
Memories dance in silver light.
Footsteps trace the silent shore,
Echoing dreams of days before.

Crisp air fills the quiet space,
Nature's breath, a soft embrace.
Shadows flicker, faint and pale,
In the stillness, stories sail.

Beneath the stars, the ice glows bright,
Time stands still, a gentle flight.
Colors bleed in twilight's hue,
Frozen tales of me and you.

The edge of night, a silver seam,
Carving paths through whispered dream.
Silent waters hold their gaze,
Reflecting hopes through winter's haze.

Memory lingers, soft and clear,
Every moment forever near.
On the icebound edge we stand,
Holding time in our own hands.

Fractured Ice

The surface cracks beneath our feet,
Shattering hints of life's deceit.
Every fracture speaks of pain,
Whispers caught in winter's chain.

Glistening shards of fractured dreams,
Piercing through the frozen seams.
Each shard a tale, both lost and found,
Echoes of a world unbound.

In the silence, secrets hide,
Gentle moments, hearts collide.
Crimson stains on snow-white ground,
Life's harsh truth, a bitter sound.

With every step, the ice will creak,
Tales of sorrow, fears we speak.
Yet still we walk on crystal path,
Facing storms that follow wrath.

In fractured ice, we find our way,
Resilience blooms amidst decay.
Shattered pieces, yet we rise,
In cold embrace, we find the ties.

Whispering Winds

The whispering winds through the trees,
Carry tales upon the breeze.
Secrets travel far and wide,
In gentle gusts, our dreams reside.

Rustling leaves in twilight's glow,
Echoes of the things we know.
Voices soft like distant chimes,
Carried on through space and time.

Among the mountains, winds will sing,
Of hope and joy that nature brings.
Flowing freely, never confined,
In every gust, a peace we find.

Breath of nature, pure and true,
Whispers softly, me and you.
Guiding hearts with tender grace,
In every sigh, we find our place.

Through every challenge, storm, and strife,
Winds remind us of our life.
In the chaos, calm prevails,
As whispers weave their timeless tales.

Glacial Echoes

In glaciers deep, the echoes play,
Songs of ice that never fade.
Time encased in frosty crust,
Memories linger, fade to dust.

Crystalline forms, a frozen art,
Whisper of nature, a beating heart.
Every crack, a tale untold,
Woven through the winter's hold.

Lost in silence, voices call,
Eternal dance, the rise and fall.
Glacial echoes reach the sky,
As ages pass, we hear their sigh.

In the chill, reflections gleam,
Frigid waters, a muted dream.
Beneath the surface, life abounds,
In glacial depths, the world resounds.

Echoes linger, soft and clear,
Whispers of the past draw near.
Within the ice, we find our way,
In frozen echoes, hearts will stay.

Frosted Horizons

In the dawn's cold embrace,
Whispers dance on the breeze.
Mountains draped in pure white,
Nature's art, a sweet tease.

Crystals glisten like stars,
Under the pale moon's glow.
Footsteps crunch on the path,
In the stillness, we flow.

Clouds roll over the peaks,
Veiling secrets untold.
A world wrapped in silence,
Where wonders unfold.

A canvas of frost blooms,
In soft hues of blue.
Each breath a soft cloud,
In the cold, we renew.

The horizon beckons us,
With a promise of light.
In the distance, it calls,
Guiding through the night.

A Tundra's Tale

Where the icy winds moan,
And the shadows conspire,
Lies a land of great stillness,
That sparks frozen desire.

Underneath the vast white,
Life quietly stirs.
In each hidden crevice,
Natural beauty occurs.

Whales sing from the deep,
The call of the wide sea.
Echoes rise in the tundra,
In harmonious glee.

The horizon stretches wide,
Kissed by the soft sun.
Shadows blend with the light,
As day slowly runs.

In the hush of the cold,
Stories drift in the air.
A tundra's tales whisper,
Oft forgotten, yet rare.

Beneath the Polar Veil

Beneath a sky of dreams,
Where polar bears roam free.
In shadows cast by the light,
A realm of mystery.

The dance of the aurora,
Paints the heavens so bright.
Colors swirl in the dark,
A breathtaking sight.

The frost-kissed landscape glows,
Like diamonds in the snow.
Each flake a tiny wonder,
In a world set aglow.

Whispers ride on the air,
From the deep woods nearby.
The echoes of the wild,
Where ancient spirits lie.

Embrace this frozen world,
Feel the pulse of the earth.
Beneath the polar veil,
Life's magic finds rebirth.

The Silent Flare

In the chill of the night,
A flare of light appears.
Dancing like a whisper,
Chasing away our fears.

The snowflakes gently fall,
Blanketing all in peace.
While the world holds its breath,
In quiet, sweet release.

Stars twinkle overhead,
Guiding lost hearts home.
In the vast empty space,
Together, we shall roam.

The silhouettes of trees,
Stand like guardians bold.
In their branches, secrets,
Of the night, they hold.

As the silent flare blooms,
Hope fills the icy air.
With dreams in silver threads,
We find warmth everywhere.

Secrets of the Frost

Whispers drift upon the breeze,
In the hush where silence sleeps.
Shimmering jewels caught in trees,
Winter's secrets, softly keeps.

Frozen footprints trace the night,
Each step a story left behind.
Underneath the silver light,
Nature's heart, so pure and kind.

Icicles hang like crystal swords,
Guarding dreams in icy gates.
A world alive with frozen words,
In the stillness, fate awaits.

Beneath the frost, a fire glows,
Hidden warmth in every shard.
The chilly breath of winter blows,
Where love and solace are the guard.

In this realm of shimmering white,
The secrets of the frost remain.
Glimmers dance in soft moonlight,
In silence, whispers like the rain.

Frosted Breath

The air is thick with frosty breath,
Each exhale a ghostly sigh.
Nature dons her crystal dress,
As snowflakes fall from the sky.

Treasures glisten on the ground,
Nature's art, a grand display.
In this silence, peace is found,
Whispers of the winter day.

Each branch wears a diamond crown,
Silent sentinels of the night.
In their stillness, hopes abound,
Wrapped snugly in winter's light.

Air as sharp as crystal glass,
Breath's soft fog hangs in the air.
In this moment, time will pass,
Yet beauty lingers everywhere.

Frosted breath, a fleeting dream,
In the chill, we find our glow.
With every breath, we gently beam,
Connected in the ebb and flow.

Mirrors of the Glacial Realm

Glacial waters hold the sky,
Reflecting dreams in icy waves.
A world where fantasies can fly,
In hidden depths, the spirit braves.

Mountains rise like ancient guards,
Their faces cold, yet wise as time.
In every crack, a thousand shards,
Mirror moments, echo rhyme.

Crystallized tales from ages past,
Snow-specked wisdom, soft and bright.
The whispers of the frost will last,
Guiding hearts in the still night.

In the depths of frosted glass,
Reflections dance in frosty light.
Every shadow, every pass,
Stories shared in pure delight.

Mirrors gleam of what has been,
The glacial realm, profound and vast.
In its depth, a magic seen,
A future born from winter's past.

Silence of the Snowbound

In the hush of snowbound nights,
Whispers of the winter's grace.
Beneath the pale, enchanting lights,
The world finds its quiet space.

Snowflakes dance on icy wings,
Softly falling, gently laid.
In this stillness, the heart sings,
Wrapped in dreams that winter made.

Trees, like guardians, stand so tall,
Covered deep in nature's quilt.
In the silence, we heed the call,
Of timeless moments softly built.

Echoes of a distant past,
Cuddle close in winter's hold.
Each breath drawn in, a spell is cast,
In this cold, our hearts are bold.

The silence of the snowbound sphere,
Embraces all that we are near.
In this hush, we find our cheer,
Guided by love, we hold so dear.

Stillness in the Snow

Whispers soft beneath a gray,
Blankets hush the light of day.
Footprints vanish, secrets keep,
In the silence, shadows sleep.

Frosty air, a breath so clear,
Nature holds her heart quite near.
Snowflakes dance on winter's breath,
A gentle pause before the death.

Trees stand tall in purest white,
Guardians of the still, sweet night.
Branches bow with weighty grace,
In this quiet, we embrace.

Stars peek through the clouded veil,
Moonlight casts a silver trail.
Everything in tranquil show,
Lost in thoughts, we drift with snow.

When the dawn begins to break,
And the world starts to awake,
Stillness whispers, soft and slow,
In the magic of the snow.

Wisps of Cold Clarity

In the morning, breath exhales,
Crystal breath on icy trails.
Sunlight glints on frozen streams,
Nature's voice is soft in dreams.

Pine trees wear a coat of frost,
In this world, I'm never lost.
Every glance reveals the grace,
Of winter's pure, enchanting face.

Clouds above, so soft, so light,
Shadows dance in morning's light.
Every flake that tumbles free,
Carries whispers, deep with glee.

Beneath the glassy, tranquil skies,
Every moment slowly flies.
Nature's sigh, a breath in time,
Filling hearts with winter's rhyme.

As the daylight starts to fade,
Wisps of clarity thus laid,
In the glow of dusk's embrace,
Find the quiet, hidden space.

A Symphony of Ice

Notes of winter fill the air,
Crystal chimes beyond compare.
Branches creak, a soft lament,
In this realm, all time is spent.

Melodies of frost and snow,
Every sound a gentle flow.
Nature plays her sweet refrain,
In the cold, life starts anew again.

Echoes dance from bough to ground,
Through the stillness, hear the sound.
Sculpted shapes of nature's hand,
Frozen beauty, cold and grand.

When the sun dips low and shy,
Colors blend across the sky.
Harmony in every tone,
In this symphony, we're not alone.

As the night begins to fall,
Stars awaken, hear the call.
In the heart of winter's might,
Find the magic in the night.

The Calm Before Thaw

In the hush of winter's breath,
Time hangs still, a dance with death.
Nature waits with bated breath,
As we linger, love bequeath.

Underneath the layer cold,
Life lies waiting, secrets hold.
Tension builds, a silent plea,
In this pause, we yearn to be.

Colors fade to muted gray,
Yet the promise won't decay.
Soon the warmth will melt the ice,
In this stillness, we think twice.

Clouds gather, whispers of change,
Softly hint of paths deranged.
Hope resides within the chill,
In the quiet, hearts are still.

When the thaw begins to stir,
Life returns, the peace a blur.
Yet for now, let stillness reign,
In this calm, we feel the strain.

When Stars Meet Snow

In the silent night they gleam,
Stars whisper dreams as they beam.
Snowflakes dance in the chill,
Nature's wonders, a magic thrill.

Underneath the silver light,
Fields of white, a pure delight.
Footprints trace a path unknown,
As the world turns to stone.

The sky paints a crystal show,
While frosty breezes gently blow.
Hearts feel warm, despite the cold,
As stories of wonder unfold.

Every twinkle tells a tale,
Of love that prevails, without fail.
In this serene, enchanting glow,
When stars meet the silent snow.

Beyond the Icy Veil

Hidden worlds beneath the frost,
In shadows long, so much is lost.
Nature's breath, a whisper fine,
Beneath the surface, secrets shine.

Glistening shards, a crystal sheet,
Every crack, a story sweet.
The air is still, the moonlight strange,
In this vast realm, all seems to change.

Windswept paths of glimmering might,
Invite the brave to dream tonight.
With every step, hearts race and soar,
Towards wonders unseen, forevermore.

Echoes murmur through the night,
Of ancient tales bathed in light.
Beyond the veil where dreams congeal,
Lies the truth of the icy reel.

The Heart of the Frozen North

In the depths where silence reigns,
Snowflakes fall like soft refrains.
Mountains stand with stoic grace,
Guardians of this frozen space.

Beneath the stars so crystal clear,
Whispers of the wild we hear.
Every breath, a frosty sigh,
In the heart where spirits fly.

Arctic winds weave tales of old,
Of legends fierce, and hearts bold.
Icebergs drift like floating dreams,
In this land of endless themes.

Eagles soar through skies of grey,
In the frozen north, where night meets day.
Adventure calls in glacial hues,
To those who seek, the heart renews.

Firelight dances, shadows play,
In every corner, night and day.
The heart beats strong, a rhythmic roar,
In the embrace of the frozen floor.

A Tapestry of Icicles

Hanging like diamonds, pure and bright,
Icicles shimmer in pale moonlight.
Nature's artwork, delicate, fair,
Each one a treasure, beyond compare.

Threads of frost weave tales untold,
In each sharp edge, stories unfold.
Beneath the eaves, they shimmer and sway,
A tapestry brightening the grey.

As winter breathes its gentle sigh,
Colors of nature, a lullaby.
The world transformed, a crystal scene,
Where every moment whispers serene.

Step lightly on the frozen ground,
Where magic and wonder abound.
With every glimmer, a promise grows,
In this world where serenity flows.

As dawn breaks, the sun will rise,
Melting treasures beneath the skies.
Yet memories linger, soft and cold,
In the tapestry of icicles, bold.

Twilight in the Tundra

The sun dips low, the shadows creep,
Whispers of night where silence sleeps.
Colors blend in a soft embrace,
A canvas drawn with gentle grace.

Crisp air lingers, a bite so slight,
Fading warmth of departing light.
Crystalline stars begin to glow,
A glimmering hope in the snow.

Footprints fade on the powdery ground,
Echoes of nature's heartbeat found.
Stillness reigns, yet life still teems,
In twilight hours, we can dare to dream.

The horizon blushes, a fleeting show,
As icy winds begin to blow.
The world transforms in shades so grand,
An ethereal beauty at winter's hand.

Underneath the vast, starlit dome,
In the tundra's arms, we find our home.
As night unfolds with a gentle sigh,
We find our peace beneath the sky.

Frostbitten Memories

Sitting by the fire's warm glow,
I recall the tales of long ago.
Whispers of laughter, warmth, and cheer,
In frosty air, they still feel near.

Each breath a cloud in the crisp night,
Ghosts of our past in the pale moonlight.
Echoes of voices in the frost,
Things we cherished, never lost.

Snowflakes waltz as they gently fall,
Painting the world like a soft white shawl.
Memories swirl in the chilly breeze,
Through frozen woods, they drift with ease.

I close my eyes, let time unwind,
In every flake, a piece I find.
Frostbitten moments that won't decay,
In winter's grasp, forever stay.

As the embers fade into the night,
The warmth of love remains so bright.
Through every season, far or near,
Frostbitten memories, forever dear.

Glimmering in the Gloom

In shadows deep, a spark ignites,
A shimmer bright in the endless nights.
Through tangled trees and icy streams,
Glimmers of hope weave through our dreams.

The moonlight dances on frosted leaves,
Whispered secrets that nature weaves.
Stars peek out, tiny and bold,
In the chill, their stories unfold.

Footfalls soft on the whispering ground,
Lost in the light that cannot be found.
Yet, through the darkness, a glow remains,
A promise whispered in silver chains.

Gloom may settle, heavy and thick,
Yet within it lies every flick.
A tapestry woven with courage and grace,
In the heart of shadows, we find our place.

So let us walk where the shadows play,
Finding the glimmers that guide our way.
For in the night, though dark and deep,
Hope's gentle light is ours to keep.

The World in White

A blanket soft drapes the ground,
In hushed silence, peace is found.
Every branch adorned with ice,
Nature's beauty, pure and nice.

Footprints trace where children laugh,
Creating memories in the aftermath.
Snowball fights and sleds that glide,
In winter's magic, hearts open wide.

Soft flakes tumble from skies so gray,
Each moment cherished in its play.
Shimmering lights on houses glow,
Welcoming warmth in the winter snow.

As night descends, the stars align,
The world in white, a perfect design.
Our dreams take flight on this frozen sea,
In a landscape kissed by serenity.

So let us wander through this land,
Where joy and love go hand in hand.
In every flake, a story bright,
We embrace the wonder of the world in white.

Under the Polar Sky

Under the vast polar dome,
The silence whispers, cold and clear.
Stars like diamonds softly roam,
In the night, their light so dear.

Snowflakes fall like gentle dreams,
Carpeting the world in white.
Moonlight dances on icy streams,
Painting shadows, soft and bright.

The air is crisp, a breath of frost,
Nature's canvas, pure and wide.
In this realm, no love is lost,
Under the sky, we take pride.

Beneath the auroras' bright display,
Colors swirl in a cosmic dance.
Hours drift, then fade away,
In this beauty, we find our chance.

Together here, we face the cold,
Wrapped in warmth, we hold on tight.
Stories of old will now be told,
Under the polar sky so bright.

Radiance on Ice

Upon the lake, a blanket glows,
Radiance shining, pure and bold.
Every ripple, a secret shows,
Whispers of moments yet untold.

Glistening shards in morning's light,
Each step crunches beneath our feet.
Nature's jewels, a dazzling sight,
In this world, our hearts do meet.

Glaciers gleam with ancient grace,
Time's embrace, a frozen tale.
We find solace in this space,
Where the sun and shadows sail.

Beneath the arch of azure skies,
We chase the warmth of fleeting rays.
In the stillness, a love that flies,
Through winter's chill, our spirits blaze.

Here, in the aura all around,
Ice and warmth in loyalty blend.
In the radiance, peace is found,
On this journey, with you, my friend.

Chilling Reflections

In the mirror of the lake,
Worlds collide in quiet grace.
Every breath a gentle quake,
Nature's beauty, a soft embrace.

Mountains stand with crowns of snow,
Guardians of this tranquil land.
With each whisper, cold winds blow,
Secrets held within their hand.

Reflections dance, shadows play,
A timeless waltz on sapphire seas.
Days like this hold care at bay,
Wrapped in winter's sweet surcease.

Here, we pause to drink the air,
Sipping silence, pure and deep.
Moments linger, still and rare,
In the chilling arms of sleep.

As twilight casts its dusky veil,
Stars emerge from their cozy beds.
In this spell, forever frail,
Chilling reflections weave our threads.

Frost's Gentle Heart

In the heart of winter's grasp,
A tender warmth begins to bloom.
Frost, like velvet, seeks to clasp,
The beauty found in nature's room.

Leaves wear crystals, pure and bright,
As dawn unveils the waking day.
In every flake, a ray of light,
Painting the world in soft array.

A gentle hush blankets the ground,
In this stillness, peace we find.
Each soft whisper, a sacred sound,
Frost's embrace, forever kind.

Together, we wander this land,
Through fields of white, so vast and true.
In every step, we understand,
Nature's heart beats close to you.

As night descends, the moon takes flight,
Casting silver upon the ground.
In frost's gentle heart, pure delight,
A world of dreams in silence found.

The Last Light of Dusk

The sun dips low in the sky,
Painting whispers in gold,
The world slows down to sigh,
As shadows begin to unfold.

A gentle breeze starts to glide,
Carrying secrets untold,
Night's blanket begins to slide,
Over the fields of marigold.

Stars awaken, shy and bright,
In the canvas of twilight,
Each flicker, a distant flight,
Dancing in the silent night.

The moon peeks with a grin,
Casting dreams on the lake,
In the stillness, we begin,
To awaken hearts that ache.

Hold onto this fleeting glow,
Each moment, a memory made,
As the last light starts to go,
In the beauty, we're not afraid.

Veils of Ice

Silent whispers in the air,
Veils of ice drape the land,
Crystal wonders everywhere,
Nature's magic, finely planned.

Trees adorned with frosted breath,
Glittering under winter's gaze,
A world transformed, untouched by death,
Caught in a shimmering haze.

Each step crunches, soft and light,
Footprints trace a dance of grace,
Underneath the pale moonlight,
As stars twinkle in their place.

Embrace the chill, feel the freeze,
In the stillness, find your peace,
Nature holds us, with such ease,
In the beauty, worries cease.

Veils of ice, a fleeting scene,
Moments held in time's embrace,
Watch them fade, pristine and clean,
In the heart, forever trace.

Enigmatic Glaciers

Majestic giants stand so tall,
Guardians of the ancient past,
Their icy forms, a silent call,
Whispers of the ages cast.

Secrets lie in every crevice,
Stories written in the frost,
Nature's art, in every premise,
Tales of what was gained and lost.

Light refracts in hues of blue,
Melting slowly with the sun,
Every drop, a world anew,
In the cycle we are one.

Time entwined in glacier's flow,
Each layer tells of storms endured,
Beauty born from nature's woe,
In stillness, our hearts are lured.

Embrace the lessons held so dear,
In the ice, find warmth and grace,
As enigmas reappear,
In nature's vast and wild space.

Distant Horizons

Clouds drift softly, shadows play,
Where land meets the ocean's hue,
Horizons stretch, a vast array,
Whispers of dreams come into view.

Seagulls call with carefree flight,
Breezes carry tales of roam,
On the edge of day and night,
A promise of distant home.

Waves crash softly on the shore,
Rhythms of a timeless song,
In their dance, we seek for more,
Lessons of where we belong.

Sunsets paint a grand farewell,
Casting gold across the sea,
In that magic, hearts can swell,
With the hopes of what can be.

As we gaze at distant sights,
Let our spirits soar and free,
For in dreams and in our flights,
We find the place we long to be.

Glacial Dreams

In the stillness of the night,
Icebergs gleam in pale moonlight.
Fragments of thoughts drift like snow,
In glacial dreams, where shadows flow.

Cold winds whisper tales untold,
Of icy realms and hearts so bold.
Frozen visions dance and sway,
In the crystal night, we lose our way.

Echoes of silence fill the air,
Harsh and sweet, beyond compare.
Each breath a cloud, a fleeting breath,
In these dreams, we flirt with death.

Stars shimmer in a frosty sky,
As dreams of winter softly fly.
A world encased in chilly grace,
In glacial dreams, we find our place.

Time drips slow, like melting ice,
Each moment lost, a heavy price.
Yet in this realm, we feel alive,
In glacial dreams, our spirits thrive.

Shimmering Silence

In a world of soft white gleam,
Silence wraps us like a dream.
Every crystal holds a thought,
In shimmering silence, we are caught.

Footsteps echo, slight and sure,
Ghosts from ages, we endure.
A blanket thick, a whispers's grace,
In the snow's embrace, we find our place.

Beneath the frost, the earth breathes low,
Secrets hidden in winter's glow.
The frosted trees, they stand so tall,
In shimmering silence, we hear their call.

Moonlight dances on the ice,
A fleeting moment, pure and nice.
Every twinkle, a tender sigh,
In silence wrapped, we learn to fly.

Time stands still in this enchanted haze,
Lost in the beauty, we muse and gaze.
In the stillness, our spirits enhance,
In shimmering silence, we find our chance.

Whispering Winds of Ice

Whispering winds around me blow,
Carrying tales of ice and snow.
Each gust a voice, so softly told,
Secrets of winter, fierce and bold.

Crystals glisten on every branch,
Nature's beauty in a trance.
Through frozen forests, hearts ignite,
Whispering winds, in the quiet night.

A chorus swells, both fierce and fair,
Echoed softly in the frigid air.
Every swirl holds a soft embrace,
In the night's grip, we find our space.

Call of the wild, so deep and clear,
In icy breath, we feel no fear.
Lost in the music of nature's weave,
In whispering winds, we learn to believe.

The stars twinkle where shadows dance,
In the vastness, we find our chance.
While the world sleeps under ice so wise,
Whispering winds carry our sighs.

Frostbitten Memories

Frostbitten memories fade like mist,
In the chill, our hearts persist.
Each moment frozen, carved in time,
Whispers of laughter, a distant chime.

Under starlit skies, we remember,
Glowing embers of a defiant ember.
The taste of joy, the sting of pain,
In frostbitten memories, love's refrain.

Ghostly figures pace the ground,
In every silence, echoes resound.
We dance through dreams on frozen lakes,
Frostbitten memories, the heart awakes.

The winter winds carry us afar,
Beneath the blanket of a silver star.
Each sigh of frost, a story to tell,
In frostbitten memories, we dwell.

Yet with spring, we yearn to be free,
To thaw the heart's cold jubilee.
But in the chill, we still can see,
Frostbitten memories, you and me.

Polar Night's Embrace

Underneath the starry shroud,
Whispers float in icy air.
A world cloaked in a heaviness,
Silence reigns, a solemn pair.

Moonlight dances on the snow,
Casting shadows, soft and bright.
The chill wraps around like dreams,
In the depths of polar night.

Each breath is seen like silver clouds,
Nature holds her breath in peace.
Timeless moments slip away,
In this frozen, sweet release.

Awaiting dawn's gentle caress,
Stars begin to fade and wane.
The heartbeats echo through the cold,
In the night's soft, tender reign.

Dancing flames of distant fires,
Twinkling lights in windows glow.
Inside, warmth and kindness reign,
While outside it continues snow.

The Still Light of Winter

Morning breaks with a gentle hush,
Frosted branches, pure delight.
A stillness wrapped in silver hues,
The world beneath the white.

Footprints trace a lonesome path,
Crystals sparkle in the sun.
Every breath is a fleeting thought,
In this season, we are one.

Wind whispers through the barren trees,
Echoing tales of time untold.
As shadows lengthen, daylight wanes,
A chill descends with evening's fold.

But warmth still lingers in our hearts,
Gathered close in silent cheer.
The still light of winter calls,
To treasure moments we hold dear.

Under stars that softly gleam,
Night wraps us in soft embrace.
In winter's stillness, love remains,
A sacred, timeless space.

Shimmering Silence

In the quiet glow of snow,
Where whispers cradle the night.
Stars above like scattered pearls,
Shimmering in pure delight.

A canvas painted white and blue,
Nature breathes in frozen grace.
Each flake a fleeting masterpiece,
Falling with a tender trace.

Bare branches reach for twilight's kiss,
Crisp air sings a secret song.
In this stillness, we find peace,
Where the heart feels it belongs.

The world holds its breath in awe,
Wrapped within a silent vow.
To cherish moments soft and fleeting,
In serenity's timeless now.

As night extends its velvet cloak,
Moonlight spills on fields so bright.
In shimmering silence we reside,
Adrift in wonder, pure delight.

Shadows Beneath the Ice

Beneath the glassy surface lies,
Whispers of the ancient past.
Memories held in frozen depths,
A world trapped, shadows cast.

Creeping currents weave their tales,
Life stirs in this hidden place.
Nature's rhythm beats below,
In a delicate, tender pace.

Each crack tells stories long forgotten,
In the stillness, secrets glow.
Echoes of a time unveiled,
In shadows beneath the snow.

Crisp air sharpens every sound,
The icy surface shimmers bright.
Yet, there's warmth in gathering dark,
A dance within the fading light.

Beneath the weight of winter's grip,
Life pulses, soft yet strong.
In the shadows, we find beauty,
Where the silent spirits throng.

Echoes of Frozen Dreams

In the still of winter's grasp,
Whispers dance on icy air.
Shadows cast by silvery light,
Dreams entombed with gentle care.

Footsteps crunch on crystal paths,
Where silence reigns like quiet snow.
Echoes of a world once warm,
Fleeting memories strung in glow.

Frosted breath hangs in the night,
Painting stories on the ground.
Each exhale, a fleeting spark,
In this realm where dreams are found.

A moonlit sky, a tranquil sight,
Caressing branches draped in white.
In this kingdom, time stands still,
Life awaits with a patient thrill.

Frozen dreams weave tales of old,
In every flake, a fragment told.
Hearts encased in winter's spell,
In echoes deep, we bid farewell.

Luminous Landscapes

Dawn breaks over hills of white,
Casting hues of softest gold.
Sparkling crystals, pure delight,
A world wrapped in blankets bold.

Footsteps trace the morning light,
In valleys deep where shadows play.
Nature's brush paints scenes so bright,
Awakening the dreams of day.

Gentle breezes, whispers sweet,
Carry tales of nature's grace.
Each moment, a fleeting treat,
In this bright, enchanting space.

Mountains rise like ancient kings,
Crowned in frost, they stand so grand.
Luminous, the silence sings,
In this vast and wondrous land.

Below, the rivers gleam with cheer,
Reflecting skies of endless blue.
Luminous, they draw us near,
To embrace the beauty true.

Frigid Hues

In a world of frigid hues,
Where sunlight flickers thin and shy.
Colors blend in frosty views,
Like paintings brushed beneath the sky.

A canvas stretched in icy breath,
Blues and whites in harmony.
Dancing shades, they whisper death,
To summer's warmth, a memory.

Glacial tongues stretch far and wide,
Clutching secrets deep below.
In their grip, life does abide,
A frozen tale, a hushed echo.

Every flake a story told,
In patterns unique, they unfurl.
A beauty carved from the cold,
Capturing the heart of the world.

Beneath the frost, life blooms anew,
In resilient hues of soft rebirth.
From silence, whispers break on through,
Frigid colors breathe with mirth.

Snowbound Whispers

Snowflakes fall like gentle sighs,
Blanketing the world in peace.
Whispers travel through the skies,
Where winter's grasp will never cease.

Every branch adorned in white,
Nature dressed in purest gown.
Silent nights bring soft delight,
Crystals falling without sound.

In this realm, all hearts align,
With the magic softly spun.
Snowbound whispers, so divine,
Heralding the night begun.

Through the pines, a gentle breeze,
Carries stories far and wide.
In the hush, the heart finds ease,
Wrapped in winter's tender pride.

As the stars begin to gleam,
Light dances on each snowy peak.
Lost in a snowbound dream,
Whispers echo, soft and weak.

Luminescent Shadows

Beneath the trees, soft whispers gleam,
Shadows flicker, dance, and dream.
Moonlight kisses the silken night,
Stars awaken, a wondrous sight.

Echoes of secrets, stories untold,
In the dark, the brave feel bold.
Gentle light weaves through the gloom,
Embracing all in nature's bloom.

Glimmers of hope in every corner,
Born of darkness, a silent mourner.
Past and future waltz with grace,
In luminescent shadows, we find our place.

Every flicker, a tale to spell,
In beautiful silence, we dwell.
A world transformed, so deep, profound,
In each shadow, love is found.

Embrace the night with open eyes,
Where every shadow softly lies.
In the glow of the moon's embrace,
We discover life's hidden space.

Chasing Frost

Morning whispers on breathless wings,
Frosted petals wear crystal rings.
Nature's lace, delicate and bright,
Creeping softly in dawn's light.

Chasing shadows, twilight's breath,
In the chill, we conquer death.
Each moment ethereal, fleeting grace,
Frosty fingers gently trace.

Footsteps crunch on icy ground,
In this stillness, magic is found.
Whispers of winter, a soft refrain,
The world glitters under crystalline reign.

A dance of beauty, nature's art,
Frost painting dreams in every heart.
In every glimmer, a silent cause,
To cherish a world that coolly draws.

As sunlight breaks, the frost will fade,
But memories linger, never betrayed.
So we chase the chill and the spark,
Embracing frost before it departs.

A Dance of Light and Ice

In the heart of winter, calm and still,
Light and ice blend with perfect will.
A dance unfolds beneath the sun,
Where frozen dreams and warmth are spun.

Crystal prisms, dazzling bright,
Reflecting colors, pure delight.
Every shimmer tells a tale,
In this ballet, we set sail.

Gentle breezes, whispers low,
Ice-formed castles start to glow.
Nature's rhythm, soft and nice,
A swirling waltz of light and ice.

Footprints mark where moments freeze,
In this magic, find our ease.
As day gives way to starlit skies,
A truce is forged with winter's sighs.

Through the beauty, darkness shimmers,
Hope ignites, the heart remembers.
For in this dance, we courage find,
In light and ice, our souls aligned.

The Stillness of Winter

Softly falling, the snowflakes glide,
In the stillness, the world takes pride.
Whispers echo in the frosty air,
Winter's touch, a gentle snare.

Trees stand tall in snowy threads,
Nature rests as the silence spreads.
Every breath, a cloud in white,
Holding stillness, pure delight.

Footsteps muffled, as dreams unfold,
Secrets whispered, stories bold.
In the hush, where time lies still,
We find the warmth, the quiet thrill.

A blanket wraps the earth in grace,
Every corner, a peaceful space.
In the stillness, hearts can soar,
Giving way to winter's lore.

So let us linger in this embrace,
Beneath the stars, a calming place.
For in winter's hush, let's find our way,
In stillness, life learns how to play.

Breath of the Icy Dawn

Morning whispers softly cold,
As frost paints the world in white.
Each breath carries tales untold,
In the stillness, dreams take flight.

The sky blushes with a light hue,
Sunrise kisses the frozen ground.
Nature wakes, fresh and anew,
Awakening with a gentle sound.

Crystal shards in a bright array,
Glimmer like stars in the dawn.
While shadows of night fade away,
A new day begins, reborn.

Branches naked, dressed in ice,
Every glimmer, a fleeting glance.
In this moment, time feels nice,
Encouraging us still to dance.

The icy breath, a sweet embrace,
Calls us forth to explore and roam.
In the tranquil, enchanted space,
We find a fleeting sense of home.

Celestial Reflections

Beneath the stars, the lake lies still,
Mirroring the night sky's glow.
Each ripple stirs a longing thrill,
As time drifts softly, smooth and slow.

Constellations whisper their tales,
A dance of dreams so vast and wide.
In the silence, wonder prevails,
As hearts and heavens both confide.

Silver clouds drift on a quest,
Embracing shadows, layers swirl.
In chaos, we find our rest,
As starlight twinkles, soft and pearl.

The moon hangs low, a guiding friend,
Casting glimmers on the darkened shore.
In this bright realm, we can blend,
And seek the secrets evermore.

Reflections weave the night with grace,
Uniting worlds both near and far.
In tranquil beauty, we find our place,
Awash beneath the evening star.

Where Dreams & Ice Collide

In a realm where shadows play,
Frosted whispers fill the air.
Dreams and ice entwine today,
Crafting magic, light and rare.

Glistening worlds of crystal light,
Where wishes drift on frozen streams.
Every moment, a pure delight,
Made of sparkles, woven dreams.

The quiet echoes of the night,
Wrap us in a gentle hold.
In this place, hearts feel so right,
Warmth among the bitter cold.

Skies above, an azure sea,
Crystals dancing, twinkling bright.
In this dreamscape, wild and free,
We find solace in the night.

Where ice and dreams, they intertwine,
A tapestry of dusk and dawn.
In spirit's flight, we boldly climb,
To greet the day, forever drawn.

Fragments of Frost

The world adorned in icy lace,
Crisp and clear, a fleeting sight.
Fragments glimmer, nature's grace,
Whispers soft, embracing light.

Sparks of winter, so divine,
Each flake unique, a work of art.
In this moment, stars align,
We find warmth within the heart.

Branches bow with crystal crowns,
Beneath the weight of every shard.
In the beauty, wonder drowns,
As we wander, feeling marred.

Bitter winds can't steal our thrill,
For in the cold, warmth finds its way.
In every chill, a spark to fill,
As laughter molds the frigid day.

Fragments of frost, forever gleam,
Nature's canvas, bold and bright.
In the heart of winter's dream,
Frosted whispers guide our flight.

A Symphony of Snowflakes

Falling softly from the sky,
Each flake dances, oh so high.
A wonderland, pure and bright,
Whispers secrets in the light.

They twirl and spin in winter's breeze,
Creating art among the trees.
A symphony, such sweet delight,
Nature's harmony, pure and right.

In silence, they blanket the ground,
A tapestry of beauty found.
Together they weave a frosty quilt,
With every flake, new joy is built.

Children laugh, their faces aglow,
Building dreams of ice and snow.
A magical world, soft as a sigh,
As snowflakes fall from the sky.

With each gust of winter's breath,
Lies a promise, life and death.
For spring will come to melt away,
A fleeting dance, a perfect day.

Crystalline Echoes

Crystals sparkle, pure and clear,
Echoes whisper, drawing near.
Reflections in the frosty air,
Nature's beauty, beyond compare.

Each shard a story, bright and bold,
Tales of warmth in winter's cold.
Fractals glisten in the light,
A dazzling dance, a pure delight.

With every step, the world does gleam,
In crystalline, we chase our dream.
The fragile beauty makes us pause,
Nature's magic earns applause.

Through frozen woods, the whispers glide,
In icy silence, hearts confide.
Captured moments, never lost,
In shimmering echoes we pay the cost.

As twilight falls and shadows grow,
With every flake, the beauty flows.
Crystalline echoes, soft and light,
A fleeting glimpse of pure delight.

Beneath the Northern Lights

Colors dance across the sky,
Beneath the stars, we dream and sigh.
A canvas painted, bright and bold,
In whispers of green and hints of gold.

The night air sparkles, crisp and clear,
Radiant wonders drawing near.
A cosmic ballet, souls unite,
In wonderment beneath the lights.

The aurora sings a tale untold,
Of ancient myths and legends old.
A celestial guide on winter's night,
Leading hearts with sheer delight.

Frozen earth, with beauty draped,
Under heavens, dreams are shaped.
In the dance of lights, hearts soar free,
Discovering worlds that are meant to be.

As morning breaks and colors fade,
Memories linger, never weighed.
Beneath the northern lights, we find,
A glimpse of love that's intertwined.

Echoes in the Snow

Footsteps crunch on winter's floor,
Echoes linger forevermore.
Each print a tale, a story told,
In silent whispers, both warm and cold.

Snowflakes swirl, a gentle sigh,
As time flows softly, moments fly.
Echoes in the crisp white ground,
Nature's rhythm, a soothing sound.

Branches bow, with flakes adorned,
In this beauty, hearts are warmed.
The quiet hum of winter's grace,
In every flake, a tender trace.

Fires crackle, embers glow,
Stories shared, as breezes blow.
Echoes of laughter, soft and light,
Fill the air on this winter night.

As dawn awakens, shadows flee,
New footprints form, wild and free.
Echoes in the snow remain,
Whispering love through joy and pain.

Where Dreams Freeze

In the hush of night, dreams lie still,
Whispers of hope in the winter chill.
Unseen wonders, they softly gleam,
In a silent world, where dreams freeze.

Snowflakes fall from the starry skies,
Covering thoughts that drift and rise.
Cold winds carry a fragile sound,
In the stillness, lost dreams abound.

Shadows flicker with a crystal glow,
Time is frozen, emotions slow.
In the heart of winter's embrace,
A frozen moment, a timeless space.

Frosted branches, nature's art,
As winter weaves the dreams impart.
In icy realms, stillness reigns,
Where everything lost, regains its chains.

Yet within this frozen plight,
Hope shines bright, a guiding light.
For when the thaw begins to creep,
Awakens dreams, from their winter sleep.

The Frosted Mirror

A frost wraps the world in silence clear,
Each breath visible, as life draws near.
Trees clad in crystals, a beautiful sight,
Reflecting the glow of the pale moonlight.

Windows shimmer with icy lace,
Framing memories of a warm embrace.
In whispers of winter, stories unfold,
Forgotten dreams, in reflections told.

The world rests beneath a chilling sheen,
Quiet echoes of what might have been.
In this frosted mirror, we dare to see,
The shadows of who we long to be.

Time bends softly in the winter air,
As thoughts dance lightly without a care.
Imaginations flicker, like candle flames,
In the frozen glass, we call out names.

And as the dawn breaks through the night,
The mirror cracks with a golden light.
Spring will breathe life into every seam,
As we awaken from our frosted dream.

Realm of the Ice Spirits

In the realm where the ice spirits dwell,
Whispers of magic rise and swell.
Among the snowflakes, they twirl and glide,
In a frozen dance, with nowhere to hide.

Glittering crystals caught in the breeze,
The laughter of spirits is soft as leaves.
With every flurry, the world comes alive,
In this frosty domain, where shadows thrive.

Moonlight silver, etched on the ground,
Tales of the ancients echo around.
In the shimmering night, their presence is clear,
In the heart of winter, the spirits draw near.

Though cold may bite, there's warmth in their grace,
In the dance of the frost, we find our place.
With each gentle flake, a story ignites,
In the realm where the ice spirits light up the nights.

So when winter wraps you in its embrace,
Listen closely, find your own pace.
For in the stillness, magic can swell,
In the realm of ice spirits, where wonders dwell.

Dances of the Northern Lights

In the velvet sky, colors collide,
A dance of hues, in the night they glide.
Greens and purples, a cosmic ballet,
Painting the heavens, night turns to day.

From the Arctic breath, they rise and weave,
Stories of nature, urging us to believe.
In enchanted rhythms, they twist and spin,
Where silence sings, and dreams begin.

Each flicker and swirl, a tale of old,
Casting a spell with colors bold.
In the frosty embrace of winter's hold,
Northern lights dance, their beauty unfolds.

Glistening jewels in a fabric of night,
Whispers of magic, taking flight.
In the heart of the world, they ignite a flame,
In dances of lights, we call their name.

So step into wonder, beneath the skies,
Where magic lives and the spirit flies.
Beneath the northern glow, we find our way,
In the dances of lights that forever stay.

Shadows on Snow

Footprints whisper in the light,
Beneath the trees, cloaked in white.
Silent echoes softly sway,
As shadows dance at end of day.

A world asleep, wrapped in dreams,
Moonlight glimmers, silver beams.
Branches bow, the cold winds blow,
Tales are told of the snow.

Cold breaths linger in the air,
Each flake falls with gentle care.
Patterns weave on winter's ground,
In stillness, beauty can be found.

Frosty nights, a starry sky,
Whispers of the night winds sigh.
Nature's song, soft and low,
Carves its way through shadows' flow.

With each dawn, a promise glows,
Colors shift as sunlight shows.
From darkness born, bright visions flow,
Life returns to shadows on snow.

Breath of the Borealis

Dancing lights in northern skies,
Whispers weave and softly rise.
Colors blend, a cosmic dance,
Nature's canvas, in a trance.

The chill ignites a heart's delight,
Magic pulse in the dark night.
Stars awaken, dreams take flight,
Signs of wonder, pure and bright.

Glistening ribbons, green and gold,
Stories of the ancients told.
Each flicker tells of journeys far,
A wild spirit, a shining star.

Embrace the chill, let go your fears,
With every breath, release your tears.
A moment captured, a heartbeat's beat,
Among the wonders, life feels complete.

In nature's breath, we find our place,
Lost in beauty, time and space.
So gaze above, let your heart be free,
In the borealis' endless sea.

Crystal Serenity

In a realm where silence reigns,
Crystal waters hold their chains.
Mirror worlds of deep reflection,
Nature's calm, a soft affection.

Gentle ripples kiss the shore,
Whispers echo, wanting more.
Sunlight dances on the stream,
Inviting hearts to share a dream.

Mountains cradle, skies embrace,
Every moment, a sacred space.
Time flows softly, like a sigh,
In crystal serenity, we fly.

Nature's voice, a soothing song,
In her presence, we belong.
Leaves sway with a tender grace,
In this haven, we find our place.

Breathe in deeply, let it go,
In stillness, feel the flow.
Close your eyes, behold the scene,
Find your peace in silver sheen.

Chasing the Midnight Sun

Golden beams of fleeting light,
Paint the sky in hues so bright.
Day and night begin to meet,
In a dance, both wild and sweet.

Chasing whispers, time moves slow,
As the shadows start to glow.
Wonders woven in the dusk,
A moment's grace, a gentle husk.

Ocean waves caress the shore,
As the sun begins to soar.
Colors blend in a painter's brush,
As day surrenders to the hush.

In this realm of near and far,
Find your dreams beneath the stars.
Let them guide you through the night,
Chasing echoes of the light.

With each breath, time slips away,
In this magic, love will stay.
Hold it close, let your heart run,
Forever chasing the midnight sun.

The Frozen Mirror

In the depths of winter's grasp,
Shadows dance on crystal glass.
Whispers ride the biting wind,
Silent tales that never end.

Trees adorned in frosty lace,
Reflecting nature's quiet grace.
Amidst the stillness, hearts confide,
In this realm where dreams abide.

Footsteps crunch on snow-kissed ground,
Magic cloaked in silence found.
Each breath hangs in the frosty air,
As if the world has ceased to care.

Moonlight spills on sheets of white,
Guiding wanderers through the night.
In the frozen mirror's gaze,
Hope ignites in muted blaze.

Time suspended, moments freeze,
Whispers lost in winter's breeze.
Nature's canvas, pure and bright,
Holds the secrets of the night.

Icy Serenity

Gentle falls of snowflakes swirl,
Covering the earth in pearl.
In this tranquil, frigid space,
Nature finds her soft embrace.

A stillness blankets every street,
Making time and worries meet.
Woodlands breathe in icy mist,
In this world, none can resist.

Rivers freeze with graceful art,
Reflecting peace that warms the heart.
Structures draped in shimmering glow,
Underneath the winds that blow.

Birds find refuge, nests so warm,
While others huddle, keep from harm.
In silence deep, harmony spins,
Life's melody quietly begins.

Each frosty dawn whispers hope,
Beneath the frost, all spirits cope.
Icy serenity, sweet delight,
Holds the magic of winter's night.

Fractured Landscapes

Across the hills, the shadows spread,
Fissures form where pathways tread.
In the cold, a story's writ,
Of nature's will and aching grit.

Cracks reveal the earth's deep scars,
Underneath the silent stars.
Fragmented forms hold strength within,
A pulsing heart, where life begins.

Windswept plains and icy streams,
Fractured beauty fuels our dreams.
In broken pieces, we can find,
A tapestry, both fierce and kind.

Mountains stand, steadfast and bold,
Guardians of the stories told.
Though landscapes seem in disarray,
Nature's art will find its way.

In each fissure, a lesson lays,
Strength is born in many ways.
Fractured landscapes, wild and free,
Whisper truths, inviting thee.

Portraits of Cold

Brushed in hues of silver gray,
Nature paints a frosty day.
Portraits of cold, framed in ice,
Crafted with a careful slice.

Figures dance in frozen light,
Wanderers lost in winter's night.
Each crystal peak a story tells,
Of frozen dreams and icy spells.

In this gallery of dreams unfurled,
Beauty resides in a frigid world.
Each brushstroke holds a breath of air,
Moments caught, forever rare.

Winter's embrace may feel austere,
Yet warmth lies close, held dear.
In these portraits, life weaves gold,
Sculpting love from tales of old.

So linger here, let your eyes roam,
In chilly realms, find your home.
For in the cold, connection thrives,
In the silence, each heart survives.

Frost-kissed Dreams

In the hush of winter's night,
Frosty whispers take flight.
Dreams weave through the icebound air,
Silvery shades dance without care.

Under the blanket, soft and white,
Glimmers of hope shine so bright.
Each crystal holds a secret plea,
Warming hearts like a gentle sea.

Stars twinkle in the frosty sky,
Old wishes on the wind do sigh.
Snowflakes fall like notes of grace,
Wrapping the world in a tender embrace.

Time slows in this frozen trance,
Nature calls us to take a chance.
With every flake that softly lands,
New beginnings in our hands.

As dawn breaks with a golden hue,
Frost-kissed dreams feel fresh and new.
We rise to greet the winter's kiss,
In the chill, we find our bliss.

The Language of Cold

Beneath a veil of pristine white,
The world speaks softly, day and night.
Words frozen on a breath of air,
Whispered secrets everywhere.

Frost etches tales on window panes,
Nature's script, where beauty reigns.
Each flake a letter, pure and bright,
In the silence, there's a light.

Branches bow under the weight,
Of winter's magic, still and straight.
Voices linger, crystal clear,
In the cold, we draw near.

The language of cold, a gentle touch,
Speaks to hearts that crave so much.
With every chill that sweeps the way,
We find warmth in the fray.

So let us share these frozen words,
Among the snowflakes, dreams are stirred.
In the quiet, we will be bold,
Learning the language of cold.

Echoes of the Snowstorm

Whirling winds in a frosty dance,
Echoes wrap us in a trance.
Snowflakes tumble, wild and free,
In their chaos, we find glee.

Time stands still as tempests rage,
Nature turning a stormy page.
Each gust carries a tale untold,
Of love and loss in the icy cold.

Footprints vanish in the flurry,
Leaving behind a world of hurry.
In the stillness, we hear the call,
Of the snowstorm's enchanting thrall.

Hearts entwined, we find our way,
As echoes of the storm replay.
In the depths of this blustery night,
We discover warmth, pure delight.

So let the snowstorm howling cry,
Fill our spirits, let them fly.
With every echo, love reclaims,
The softness of the snowstorm's flames.

Crystal Reflections

In the stillness of the frosty morn,
Crystal reflections, beauty borne.
Mirrors of ice, capturing light,
Every sparkle feels so right.

Windows dressed in frosted lace,
Nature's art in every space.
Dewdrops cling like whispered dreams,
As sunlight dances, softly beams.

Scrolls of snow on branches sway,
Holding stories of yesterday.
With each glance, our hearts are drawn,
To the magic of a dazzling dawn.

Beneath the blue, the world does gleam,
In this realm, we chase the dream.
With crystal reflections all around,
In winter's pulse, our joy is found.

So let us wander through the chill,
Embracing silence, feeling still.
In the shards of ice, we find our way,
To crystal reflections of today.

The Last Light of Day

The sun dips low, a ball of fire,
Casting hues that never tire.
Whispers of gold in the fading sky,
A gentle sigh as day bids goodbye.

Birds take flight, silhouettes in grace,
Chasing dreams in the twilight space.
Night's cool breath begins to sweep,
Embracing all in shadows deep.

Stars awaken, one by one,
A silent dance, the night begun.
Moonlight drapes the world in peace,
As worries fade and moments cease.

A time to reflect, to quietly muse,
In the warmth of colors we choose.
The last light of day, a fleeting glance,
A tender farewell in evening's dance.

Hold close the beauty of day's last sigh,
As dreams take flight and softly fly.
In every heartbeat, echo the sound,
Of moments cherished, lost but found.

Patterns in the Frost

Winter whispers with icy breath,
Transforming the world, a dance with death.
Patterns arise like stories told,
On windows adorned with lace-like gold.

Each flake unique, a masterpiece,
Nature's art, finding peace.
A landscape cloaked in silvery white,
Where silence reigns in the soft twilight.

Footsteps crunch on the powdered ground,
A symphony of winter's surround.
Glistening branches hold a secret still,
As the world slows down, against its will.

Breath fogs the air, ephemeral flow,
Moments captured in the gleaming snow.
Patterns etched where the sun doesn't reach,
An unseen lesson nature will teach.

As dawn breaks in golden light,
The frost retreats, a new sight.
Yet in our hearts, the beauty stays,
In patterns of frost and wintery days.

Silence of the Shadows

In the hush of night, shadows creep,
Whispers and tales in darkness deep.
The world pauses, caught in a trance,
Where silence reigns, and secrets dance.

Figures lurk in corners unseen,
Memories echo where we have been.
A soft rustle, a fleeting glance,
In the muted light, the heart's romance.

Drifting clouds above paint the sky,
As the moon watches, a silent eye.
Dreams take flight on wings of night,
Wrapped in the magic of starlit light.

The world breathes slow in twilight's embrace,
Finding solace in this hidden place.
For in the shadows, truth resides,
Where fear may falter but hope abides.

So close your eyes, let the silence speak,
In whispered tones, where the heart is weak.
For shadows hold the tales we weave,
In their still embrace, we believe.

Twilight's Embrace

As daylight fades to a dusky hue,
Twilight whispers the night anew.
Colors blend in a tender kiss,
A fleeting moment, pure and bliss.

The sky ignites in shades of fire,
Stirring the heart with deep desire.
Stars appear, shy and bright,
Guardians of dreams in the thickening night.

Crickets sing in the velvet dark,
Nature's choir, a gentle spark.
The world glows in a soft embrace,
As evening wraps us in its grace.

Feel the calm as time slows down,
In twilight's arms, the world's crown.
Every heartbeat, a rhythmic flow,
As night descends with a gilded glow.

So hold this moment, let it last,
In twilight's embrace, shadows pass.
For in this stillness, we find our way,
Through the tender veil of night and day.

An Elegy for Ice

Once bright and clear, it glimmers white,
A fragile beauty, lost from sight.
Whispers of warmth, a bitter sting,
Grief for the frost, to which we cling.

Crystals break, their shimmer fades,
In pools of warmth, the silence wades.
Echoes of winter, cold and grim,
A requiem sung on the edge of whim.

The frozen lakes, now tender streams,
Bear witness to the melting dreams.
Lost in the thaw, our memories flee,
An elegy sung for what used to be.

Frost-gilded nights now wear a shroud,
As blooms of spring poke through the cloud.
The world awakens, but we lament,
For icy visions and moments spent.

In the heart of change, we find our peace,
Embracing the warmth, yet feel the crease.
Time drifts along, remnants of cold,
A story of ice in echoes told.

Shadows Beneath the Snow

Beneath the white, the shadows creep,
Secrets in silence, still and deep.
Ghosts of the past in quiet halls,
Echoes of laughter, now mere calls.

Footsteps muffled, whispers lost,
Memories frozen, counting the cost.
Night covers all with a gentle hand,
While beneath the surface, dreams expand.

The weight of darkness, soft as a sigh,
Where worries linger, and spirits fly.
Hushed in the glow of moonlit nights,
Shadows dance under pale, silver lights.

Each flake that falls, a tale to tell,
Of love and loss in a frozen shell.
Buried beneath, the heartbeats fade,
In shadows where once our hopes were laid.

As springtime whispers, the shadows flee,
Revealing the world in vibrant glee.
Yet in our hearts, where warmth may grow,
We hold the shadows beneath the snow.

Elysium of Frost

In the realm where silence reigns,
Beneath the frost, the beauty remains.
Delicate patterns on windows gleam,
An ethereal world, like a waking dream.

Glacial gardens with sculptures of ice,
Nature's art, a wonder device.
Each breath released, a crystal plume,
In this sanctuary, winter's bloom.

Frozen whispers fill the air,
A secret language, soft and rare.
Snowflakes drift with gentle grace,
In their descent, a timeless embrace.

The stars are twinkling, the skies so vast,
In this Elysium, shadows cast.
Where silence reigns, and hearts aspire,
To touch the chill of winter's fire.

Yet fleeting is this hallowed ground,
As thaws approach, the change resounds.
Hold dear the moments, let them stay,
In the Elysium of frost, we pray.

The Tapestry of Cold

Woven threads of winter's breath,
Crafting tales of silence and death.
A tapestry spun with silver strands,
Where frost weaves dreams with icy hands.

Each snowflake falls, a story told,
In the landscape of white, a beauty bold.
Nature's artistry, both fierce and fine,
Embroidered in patterns, a cold design.

Morning light breaks on frozen ground,
While whispers of winter echo around.
Branches are laced in glimmering hue,
In this tapestry, life feels new.

Gentle sighs as the cold winds blow,
An endless dance, a fervor flow.
Through glens and valleys, peace unfolds,
In the woven grace of the tapestry of cold.

As spring approaches, the fabric thins,
Yet through memories, the chill still spins.
A story of seasons, thread by thread,
The tapestry woven, where all is fed.

Nocturnal Glimmers

In the silence of night, stars softly gleam,
Whispers of shadows, a flickering dream.
Moonbeams caress the darkened tree,
Awakening secrets, setting them free.

The breeze carries tales of forgotten lore,
Dancing through branches, forevermore.
Creatures of night begin their ballet,
Under the watch of the Milky Way.

Gentle reflections on a still, dark lake,
Glimmers of silver, making hearts quake.
Ripples of time flow beneath the sky,
Echoes of midnight, as moments pass by.

In the depth of the woods, shadows play,
Secrets unravel in a mystic sway.
Stars seem to wink, sharing their light,
Nocturnal glimmers, pure and bright.

The dawn whispers softly, bidding goodbye,
As shades start to fade beneath the sky.
Yet in the heart, the night lingers still,
Holding its magic, a timeless thrill.

White Whisperings

Snowflakes fall with a delicate grace,
Veiling the world in a soft, white embrace.
Silence blankets the earth's weary sigh,
In the hush of the night, the whispers comply.

Trees stand adorned in a glistening lace,
Branches bow gently, as if in a trace.
Footsteps are muffled, the world feels at rest,
Wrapped in white wonder, nature's behest.

Icicles dangle like crystal chandeliers,
Reflecting the light, erasing our fears.
The air carries magic, a delicate tune,
A song of the winter beneath the pale moon.

Children's laughter dances in the chill,
As snowmen arise, with warmth to instill.
Fireplaces crackle, a glow in the night,
White whisperings echo, pure delight.

With every flake that drifts down from above,
Hearts grow warmer, wrapped in love.
As the night fades to dawn's gentle play,
White whisperings softly guide our way.

Chronicles of Chill

Frost wraps the windows, a delicate frost,
Paths that once murmured, now silent and lost.
Breath visible, like a ghost of the past,
Moments linger, too precious to last.

The world wears a cloak of glimmering white,
As shadows stretch long, welcoming night.
In each drifting flake, a tale to unfold,
Chronicles of chill, in silence retold.

The howl of the wind sings through the trees,
A melody haunting, carried by breeze.
Nature's own canvas, a story in hues,
Whispers of winter, in shades of the blues.

By the fire's glow, we gather to share,
Memories wrapped in the chill of the air.
Feet tucked in blankets, hearts open wide,
Chronicles weave, as we linger inside.

As night deepens further and stars start to gleam,
We honor the chill with each heartfelt dream.
For in every season, there's beauty to find,
Chronicles of chill, forever entwined.

Beneath Pale Skies

Beneath pale skies, where the shadows reside,
Whispers of twilight softly collide.
A canvas of colors, fading to gray,
As day gently sighs, and night finds its way.

Gentle winds carry the scent of the earth,
Revealing the secrets that linger with mirth.
The horizon blushes, bidding adieu,
To moments of light, as night hatches new.

Stars twinkle shyly, like gems in the dark,
Drawing us closer, igniting the spark.
While the moon takes its throne, regal and wise,
We wander through dreams, 'neath those pale skies.

In the quiet of dusk, reflections take flight,
Cradled in shadows, we welcome the night.
Each heartbeat echoes a gentle embrace,
Beneath pale skies, we find our own place.

As the world spins onward, in cycles we trust,
We gather our hopes, in the darkness, we must.
For every sunset brings forth a new rise,
And life dances on, beneath pale skies.

Frozen Stories

In winter's grasp, tales unfold,
Silent whispers, secrets told.
Icicles hang from every bough,
Nature's canvas, still and low.

Footprints linger on the ground,
Echoes lost, yet so profound.
Each flake dances, soft and light,
Capturing moments, holding tight.

Old trees stand, their branches bare,
Guarding dreams that linger there.
Snowflakes fall like gentle sighs,
Crafting stories 'neath gray skies.

A child's laughter fills the air,
Snowballs fly without a care.
Frozen smiles, warm hearts glow,
In this world of white and snow.

As shadows stretch and daylight fades,
Nighttime brings its silvery shades.
Stars above, a twinkling show,
In this realm where wonders grow.

Flickers in the Frost

Softly glows the morning light,
Frosty fields in pure delight.
Crystals spark where sunlight spills,
A charming scene that time distills.

Breath of winter, crisp and clear,
Flickers dance and disappear.
Over hills, the mist will rise,
Painting beauty in the skies.

Frozen ponds, a mirrored view,
Reflecting dreams of skies so blue.
Whispers carried by the breeze,
Nature's song that aims to please.

Underneath the blanket white,
Creatures scurry, hearts alight.
In the stillness, life persists,
Emerging from the morning mists.

As daylight wanes, shadows sigh,
The vibrant hues of dusk draw nigh.
Each flicker, a fleeting art,
Echos held in winter's heart.

Nature's Icy Palette

A splash of white, a hint of gray,
Nature paints in hues of play.
Frosted branches, a glistening dream,
Where sunlight winks and shadows beam.

Crimson berries peek through snow,
Bright against the world below.
Picturesque and finely brushed,
An artist's hand in winter's hush.

Clouds of fluff drift through the day,
While chilly winds begin to sway.
Every flake, a work of art,
Whispered beauty, nature's heart.

Frozen rivers, still and deep,
Guarding secrets that they keep.
Mirrored skies in icy streams,
Capturing all our hopes and dreams.

When dusk arrives, a resplendent show,
The palette shifts with twilight's glow.
In the stillness, color reigns,
Nature's icy hues remain.

Still Waters

Still waters freeze beneath the sun,
Reflecting all the things we've done.
In quiet moments, thoughts arise,
Captured in the mirror of the skies.

Hidden depths of tranquil blue,
Whispers of the past come through.
Ripples dance upon the surface,
Time unfolds in silent verses.

Snowflakes gently touch the ground,
All around, stillness found.
Nature pauses, breath held tight,
A canvas bright with purest light.

Amidst the calm, a world unfolds,
Stories waiting to be told.
In the tranquility of the morn,
Life awakens, softly born.

Silence reigns, the world breathes deep,
While echoes of the past we keep.
In still waters, truth resides,
Flowing gently, like the tides.

Chilled Minds

Thoughts drift like snowflakes in the air,
Fragile dreams beyond compare.
In the quiet, minds take flight,
Chilled indeed, but filled with light.

Winter's chill can spark a fire,
In the heart, a warm desire.
Ideas dart like stars at night,
Casting shadows, pure delight.

Amidst the frost, we ponder deep,
Chasing visions while we sleep.
Frozen moments, thoughts collide,
In the silence, worlds abide.

Books lay open, pages turn,
From each corner, passions burn.
With chilled minds, we find our way,
Through the night and into day.

In winter's grasp, we forge our dreams,
Crafting life in silver beams.
Though the air is cold and light,
Our hearts remain forever bright.

Milton Keynes UK
Ingram Content Group UK Ltd.
UKHW010231111224
452348UK00011B/659

9 789916 793916